Growing
Stronger
ADVANCED

GROWING STRONGER

A handbook for maturing Christians

John C. Souter

Tyndale House
Publishers, Inc.
Wheaton, Illinois

OTHER BOOKS BY THE AUTHOR:
Personal Bible Study Notebook Volume 1
Personal Bible Study Notebook Volume 2
Personal Prayer Notebook
Youth Bible Study Notebook
Thessalonians: A Study from The Living Bible
Jesus the Liberator
The Pleasure Seller
Grow! A Handbook for New Christians
How to Grow New Christians
A Family Hour Notebook, Getting to Know God

Unless otherwise noted, all Scripture quotations
are taken from the New American Standard Bible.

Library of Congress Catalog Card Number 79-92172.
ISBN 0-8423-1234-X, paper.
Copyright © 1980 by John C. Souter.
All rights reserved.
First printing, February, 1980.
Printed in the United States of America.

CONTENTS

Introduction 7
Getting Started 9
One **Your Self-Image 20**
Two **How to Handle Authority 38**
Three **Understanding Yourself 57**
Four **Knowing God's Will 85**
Five **Learning to Love 101**
Six **Sharing Your Faith 115**

INTRODUCTION

Welcome to Growing Stronger, Advanced. By now you have either finished Growing Stronger, Basic, or because of your knowledge and maturity you are ready to skip that book and begin this half of your Christian growth course.

This book will be of little value to you unless you have a discipler to lead you through it. (He has a manual too, called How to Grow Strong Christians.) A discipler is a spiritual Christian who has learned to apply the concepts contained in this manual. If you do not have one to work with you, ask your pastor if he can recommend someone who might be willing to help you grow.

There are six sections in this book. Your discipler will take you through this material using projects. Each project will be different. Many involve Bible study, some require memorization of a verse or two, others ask you to learn basic Christian terms. Some projects involve practical activities such as meeting other people and helping them.

You will also read selected chapters from other Christian books and be asked to report on what you learn. Look on these assignments as opportunities to build your personal library with tools that will make you more effective in God's hands. The Bible studies in this manual are based on the <u>New American Standard Bible</u>.

Try to meet with your discipler once a week. This may not always be possible, but make it your goal. At each meeting he will go over what you have learned and assign new projects. You will have opportunities to ask questions and share the experiences God has brought into your life during the week.

Don't skip ahead in this manual. Do only those tasks that have been assigned. Don't expect to move on to the next section until you have mastered previous material. If there are areas of your life in which you are fighting major sin battles, your discipler will give you additional help. Trust God to use him to bring you to spiritual maturity. Share both your problems and victories with him.

It is not enough to fill out the blanks in this manual. You must develop and practice godlike character to become a true disciple of Jesus Christ. Your goal is to <u>apply</u> the principles from each of the chapters in this book. As you work in this manual, concentrate on coming closer to God.

May God richly bless you as you begin this exciting adventure of growing to be like Jesus Christ.

GETTING STARTED

COUNTING THE COST
This manual will cost you. It will cost you hours of hard work, days of spiritual struggle, and months of persistent effort. Before you begin, be like the man who sits down to count the cost. (See Matthew 14:26-35.) Is it worth it? Do you have the time? Are you willing to make the time? Are you willing to sacrifice other things in your schedule so that you will have time? If you love the Lord Jesus and truly want to be his servant, this program is what you need.

Growth takes work, and you may want to give up when the going gets rough. But life's always a struggle. If anything is easy, it is usually not worthwhile. Make up your mind early that you are going to finish this book—that you are going to master its contents.

There will be days when you think that your discipler does not know what he is doing. There will be times when he will ask you to do things you think are a waste of time. But remember, you are asking God to use him to lead you into discipleship, and you can count on the road being rough. Make Ephesians 4:15 your goal: "We are to grow up in all aspects into Him, who is the head, even Christ."

If you are willing to pay the price of true growth, read the following statement in your discipler's presence and make your commitment to God.

COMMITMENT NO. 1
"I have counted the cost of becoming a true disciple of Jesus Christ. I realize that this commitment will cost me time and work. I also realize that there will be times when I will have to sacrifice my own pleasure in order to fulfill this commitment to grow. Before God and my discipler I announce that one of my highest priorities will be time spent in discipleship. I want to grow spiritually and am willing to pay the price for that growth."

_____   _____
(Your Name)   (Discipler)

_____
(Date)

OBEYING SPIRITUAL LEADERS
As you enter into a discipleship relationship with another Christian, you must know that the Bible has much to say about how we are to behave toward those in spiritual authority over us.

"Remember those who led you, who spoke the word of God to you; and considering the outcome of their way of life, imitate their faith. . . . Obey your leaders, and submit to them; for they keep watch over your souls, as those who will give an account. Let them do this with joy and not with grief, for this would be unprofitable for you" (Hebrews 13:7, 17).

Even though your discipler may not be an elder in your church, when you enter into a discipleship arrangement with him he becomes your immediate spiritual authority.

It is God's will that you be submissive to the leadership under which he places you—both secular and spiritual authority. It is not God's will that you allow yourself to be walked on, but rather that you listen to those who, by their spiritual age and experience, can help you grow. We will explore the concept of authority and the chain-of-command in depth, but for now it is important that you submit yourself to your discipler's care. You will not be able to complete this manual if you are not subject to his authority. Read and sign Commitment Number 2 in his presence.

COMMITMENT NO. 2
"It is my desire to become a disciple of Jesus Christ. I will submit to the spiritual leadership of the one discipling me and with God's power will do the projects he assigns for my spiritual growth."

_____   _____
(Your Name   (Discipler)

_____
(Date)

12

DAILY BIBLE STUDY RECORD
Each day after you study God's Word, list the passage you studied opposite the correct date below. In this way you will be able to keep track of your own consistency.

Month _____ Year _____

1 _____	22 _____	11 _____
2 _____	23 _____	12 _____
3 _____	24 _____	13 _____
4 _____	25 _____	14 _____
5 _____	26 _____	15 _____
6 _____	27 _____	16 _____
7 _____	28 _____	17 _____
8 _____	29 _____	18 _____
9 _____	30 _____	19 _____
10 _____	31 _____	20 _____
11 _____	Month _____	21 _____
12 _____	1 _____	22 _____
13 _____	2 _____	23 _____
14 _____	3 _____	24 _____
15 _____	4 _____	25 _____
16 _____	5 _____	26 _____
17 _____	6 _____	27 _____
18 _____	7 _____	28 _____
19 _____	8 _____	29 _____
20 _____	9 _____	30 _____
21 _____	10 _____	31 _____

13

DAILY BIBLE STUDY RECORD
Each day after you study God's Word, list the passage you studied opposite the correct date below. In this way you will be able to keep track of your own consistency.

Month _____ Year _____

1 _____	22 _____	11 _____
2 _____	23 _____	12 _____
3 _____	24 _____	13 _____
4 _____	25 _____	14 _____
5 _____	26 _____	15 _____
6 _____	27 _____	16 _____
7 _____	28 _____	17 _____
8 _____	29 _____	18 _____
9 _____	30 _____	19 _____
10 _____	31 _____	20 _____
11 _____	Month _____	21 _____
12 _____	1 _____	22 _____
13 _____	2 _____	23 _____
14 _____	3 _____	24 _____
15 _____	4 _____	25 _____
16 _____	5 _____	26 _____
17 _____	6 _____	27 _____
18 _____	7 _____	28 _____
19 _____	8 _____	29 _____
20 _____	9 _____	30 _____
21 _____	10 _____	31 _____

14

DAILY BIBLE STUDY RECORD
Each day after you study God's Word, list the passage you studied opposite the correct date below. In this way you will be able to keep track of your own consistency.

Month _____ Year _____

1 _____	22 _____	11 _____
2 _____	23 _____	12 _____
3 _____	24 _____	13 _____
4 _____	25 _____	14 _____
5 _____	26 _____	15 _____
6 _____	27 _____	16 _____
7 _____	28 _____	17 _____
8 _____	29 _____	18 _____
9 _____	30 _____	19 _____
10 _____	31 _____	20 _____
11 _____	Month _____	21 _____
12 _____	1 _____	22 _____
13 _____	2 _____	23 _____
14 _____	3 _____	24 _____
15 _____	4 _____	25 _____
16 _____	5 _____	26 _____
17 _____	6 _____	27 _____
18 _____	7 _____	28 _____
19 _____	8 _____	29 _____
20 _____	9 _____	30 _____
21 _____	10 _____	31 _____

15

APPOINTMENT SCHEDULE
Use this form to write down each of your appointments with your discipler.

Date	Day	Time	Place

16

APPOINTMENT SCHEDULE
Use this form to write down each of your appointments with your discipler.

Date	Day	Time	Place

WEEKLY PROJECTS

Section	Project	Date Given	Date Completed

WEEKLY PROJECTS

Section	Project	Date Given	Date Completed

WEEKLY PROJECTS

Section	Project	Date Given	Date Completed

YOUR SELF-IMAGE

INTRODUCTION
How you feel about yourself is very important in your ministry as Christ's disciple. If you don't like yourself, your appearance, or your abilities, you will have tremendous problems coping with life. This section is designed to help you see yourself from God's point-of-view. It is designed to help you clear your conscience and remove guilt that has come from past activities.

Love Yourself. ". . . we are so ingrained with the idea of self-denial, self-sacrifice and the fear of being egotistical that the admonition to love one's self seems almost a blasphemy. What then is the distinction between self-love and selfishness, between self-acceptance and egotism?

"One difficulty lies in the fact that the word self-love has a double meaning. It can mean self-acceptance as well as self-centeredness. . . .

"An example of self-love in the negative sense is illustrated by the Greek myth about Narcissus. He was a youth who, while gazing at his reflection in a well, fell in love with himself. Totally engrossed with his own image, he tumbled into the water and drowned. From this myth, the word narcissism is derived. Another Greek term for 'self' and 'love' denoting the same idea is auto-eroticism.

"Self-love used in the positive sense of self-acceptance is

the exact opposite of narcissism or auto-eroticism. It is actually a prerequisite for a step in the direction of selflessness. We cannot give what we do not possess. Only when we have accepted ourselves can we become truly selfless and free from ourselves. If, however, we have not found ourselves and discovered our own identity, then we must continually search for ourselves. The word <u>self-centered</u> aptly describes us when we revolve only around ourselves.

"To put it bluntly, <u>Whoever does not love himself is an egoist</u>. He must become an egoist necessarily because he is not sure of his identity and is therefore always trying to find himself. Like Narcissus, being engrossed with himself, he becomes self-centered."

Walter Trobisch
<u>Love Yourself</u>
InterVarsity Press

BIBLE STUDY
God's Love

Date of Studies_____

1. What do you think the phrase "God created man in His own image" means (Genesis 1:26, 27)? _____
_____
_____
_____

2. List each proof of God's love for us as individuals in Psalm 139:13-16. _____
_____
_____
_____

3. Who initiates our salvation (1 John 4:19)? _____
Why? _____
_____
_____

4. Did God require men to show an interest in salvation prior to his sending Christ to die on the cross? (See Romans 5:8.)
_____
_____
_____

5. What is God's grace for sinful men, according to Ephesians 2:4-9? _____
_____
_____

6. Why did God exercise this grace (v. 7)? _____
_____
_____

23

BIBLE STUDY
Sin and Forgiveness

Date of Studies _____

1. Summarize simply what each of the following verses tell about sin:

Isaiah 53:6 _____

Isaiah 64:6 _____

Romans 3:10 _____

Romans 3:23 _____

2. If man was created in God's image, how could he be so full of corruption in God's eyes? _____

_____

_____

3. How does God remove our sin (1 John 1:7, 9)? _____

_____

_____

4. What does God do with the sin of those who trust him (Psalm 103:10-12)? _____

_____

_____

_____

5. What is God's goal for us through Christ (2 Corinthians 5:21)? _____

_____

_____

BIBLE STUDY
The Self-Image

Date of Studies_____

1. Summarize Jesus' self-confidence in these verses:

John 8:58 _____

John 10:30 _____

John 14:9 _____

Philippians 2:6-8 _____

_____

2. Was Jesus confident in his own identity or did he reveal poor self-acceptance? _____

_____

3. Could Jesus have ministered to others so effectively if he had not loved himself? _____

_____

_____

4. How did Jonathan love David (1 Samuel 18:1)? _____

_____

5. How are we to love others (Galatians 5:14; James 2:8)?

_____

_____

6. Do these verses say we are to love others <u>instead</u> of ourselves?_____ What do they indicate our attitude toward ourselves should be? _____

_____

_____

25

BIBLE STUDY
The Self-Image

Date of Studies_____

7. Extract any teaching on the self-image in the following references:

   a. Ephesians 5:28 _____
   _____
   _____

   b. Ephesians 5:29 _____
   _____
   _____

   c. Ephesians 5:33 _____
   _____
   _____

8. Is there anything in the above verses which implies that we are not to love ourselves? _____
_____
_____

9. When you love yourself, are you being self-centered and egotistical? _____
_____
_____
_____

10. Does God look upon our "outer frame" or our inner person (1 Samuel 16:7; 1 Peter 3:3, 4)? _____
_____

Why? _____
_____
_____

26

BIBLE STUDY
The Self-Image

Date of Studies_____

11. Can you use your physical imperfections for God's glory (2 Corinthians 12:7-10)? _____
_____
_____

12. Should you question how God made you (Romans 9:20; Isaiah 45:9)? _____
_____
_____

13. Is there anything wrong with comparing yourself with others according to 2 Corinthians 10:12? _____
_____
_____

14. Summarize any principles about your self-image revealed in the following verses:

Proverbs 23:7 _____

Proverbs 27:19 _____

Philippians 2:13 _____

Philippians 4:8 _____

Philippians 4:13 _____

15. Summarize what the Bible teaches about your self-image. (Use the last three Bible study pages.)_____
_____
_____
_____
_____
_____

27

MEMORY WORK SHEET

Scripture Reference _____ Date _____

1. Translation to be used: _____
2. Exact passage to be memorized: _____
   _____
   _____
   _____

3. When you're ready, review the passage above and quiz yourself by writing it here: _____
   _____
   _____
   _____
   _____

4. Use this space for a second quiz of the passage: _____
   _____
   _____
   _____
   _____

5. Each time you review, list the date and check your score:

Review date	Perfect	Average	Poor
Review date_____	Perfect_____	Average_____	Poor_____
Review date_____	Perfect_____	Average_____	Poor_____
Review date_____	Perfect_____	Average_____	Poor_____
Review date_____	Perfect_____	Average_____	Poor_____
Review date_____	Perfect_____	Average_____	Poor_____
Review date_____	Perfect_____	Average_____	Poor_____

28

BIBLE STUDY
The Conscience

Date of Studies_____

1. How does the dictionary define "conscience"? _____
_____
_____
_____

2. Summarize the "type" of conscience believers are to possess in the following references:

   a. Acts 23:1_____
   _____

   b. Acts 24:16 _____
   _____

   c. 2 Timothy 1:3_____
   _____

3. What can cleanse your conscience (Hebrews 9:14)?
_____
_____

4. Is it possible to weaken your conscience and make it oversensitive so that you <u>make</u> things to be sinful (1 Corinthians 8:7; Romans 14:22, 23)?
_____
_____
_____

5. How can you keep from arousing your conscience (1 Corinthians 10:25-27) in the area of questionable things?
_____
_____
_____
_____

BIBLE STUDY
The Conscience

Date of Studies _____

6. Is it possible, on the other hand, to sear your conscience so that it no longer lets you know right from wrong? (See 1 Timothy 4:2.)

_____

_____

_____

7. What type of offenses toward other people cause your conscience to "act up"? _____

_____

_____

_____

_____

8. What will ultimately happen if a person continues in a state of spiritual rebellion? (See Titus 1:15, 16.) _____

_____

_____

_____

9. What type of behavior is Peter recommending in 1 Peter 3:16? _____

_____

_____

10. Explain the goal of our instruction in your own words (1 Timothy 1:5). _____

_____

_____

Dahlgren Methodist Church
Dahlgren, Virginia 22448

BOOK REPORT
Name of Book _____

Author _____ Publisher _____

Chapter(s) read _____

1. Chapter _____ summarized: _____
_____
_____
_____
_____
_____

2. Chapter _____ summarized: _____
_____
_____
_____
_____
_____

3. List important points you should remember: _____
_____
_____
_____
_____
_____

4. What were the most impressive facts you learned? ___
_____
_____
_____
_____
_____

TAKE A LOOK AT YOURSELF

Date_____

It is important that you discuss this sheet with your discipler before filling it out.

1. Have you ever been deeply wounded by someone?_____
_____
_____
_____

2. How do you (truthfully) feel about your parents?
_____
_____
_____
_____

3. Are there things in your past which make you feel guilty?
_____
_____
_____

4. Are there sin areas in your life which God has forgiven, but for which you cannot forgive yourself? _____
If so, what? _____
_____
_____
_____

5. Have you ever been personally rejected?_____ If yes, does it still bother you?_____
_____
_____
_____

32

TAKE A LOOK AT YOURSELF

Date_____

6. When you look in a full-length mirror, what bothers you most?_____

Why? _____

_____

_____

7. Do you compare yourself with others? _____

How do you measure up?_____

_____

_____

_____

8. Do you sometimes feel you have been short-changed in appearance or ability? _____

_____

_____

_____

9. Do you feel God has made some mistake with you?_____

If so, what? _____

_____

_____

_____

_____

10. Stop and think about it. Do you blame God for "messing up" your life? _____

_____

_____

_____

_____

RESOURCE SHEET

"What do you think when you look in a mirror? Are you satisfied with yourself? If you are, you have a healthy self-image.

"We all have an opinion of ourselves whether we spend a lot of time thinking about it or not. Our self-image is the 'map' that we consult about ourself. It is the mental picture of our self-identity. It is the 'I am' feeling of a person. We either feel good about ourself or we dislike or even hate and despise ourself.

"Where did our self-image come from and how did it develop? The image we have of ourself is built upon clusters of many memories. Very early in life we begin to form concepts and attitudes about ourself, others, and the world. Our self-concept is actually a cluster of attitudes about our self—some favorable and some unfavorable. Our mind never forgets an experience. We may not be conscious of it but it is still there."

H. Norman Wright
Improving Your Self-Image
Harvest House Publishers

COMMITMENT NO. 3

"With the Lord's strength I commit myself to _____

_____

_____

_____

_____

_____	_____
Disciple	Discipler
_____	_____
Date	Date

34

PLAN OF ATTACK
Overcoming Guilt

Date_____

Your discipler will share with you the information necessary to fill this page.

1. _____

2. _____

3. _____

4. _____

35

PLAN OF ATTACK
Developing a Clear Conscience

Date_____

Your discipler will share with you the information necessary to fill this page.

1. _____
_____
_____
_____
_____
_____
_____

2. _____
_____
_____
_____

3. _____
_____
_____

4. _____
_____
_____

5. _____
_____
_____

36

PLAN OF ATTACK
Self-Acceptance

Date_____

Your discipler will share with you the information necessary to fill this page.

1. _____

2. _____

3. _____

37

WHAT YOU'VE LEARNED

Date of Quiz_____

What have you learned in this section? This little quiz will give you an opportunity to see how much you've learned while studying the material in this chapter. Don't let this quiz worry you. Its purpose is not to give you a grade, but to show what you've learned. It will let you know in what areas you need work.

1. _____
2. _____
3. _____
4. _____
5. _____
6. _____
7. _____
8. _____
9. _____
10. _____
11. _____
12. _____
13. _____
14. _____
15. _____
16. _____
17. _____
18. _____

19. _____

20. _____

2
HOW TO HANDLE AUTHORITY

INTRODUCTION
The world is suffering from authority conflicts. Our prisons are full of inmates who do not want to have anyone tell them what to do. Our businesses are full of employees who would love to tell off the boss. A Christian must know what the Bible says about both secular and spiritual authority.

The Bible is based on the chain-of-command. God is the ultimate authority and he is the one who bestows or allows all earthly authority. Very seldom does the Bible recommend rebellion of any type—no matter how dictatorial the authority figure might be.

God wants each of us to be under authority. Before we can be parents, we must first be children. Before we can be teachers, we must first be students. Throughout life we find ourselves under the care of parents, teachers, military superiors, civil authorities, employers, and, in many cases, a husband. It is God's will that you be submissive to the leadership under which he places you—both secular and spiritual authority.

For any organization to run properly, there must be a proper relationship between those in charge and the staff. Most families, businesses, and governments suffer from a tremendous lack of loyalty from those who are under authority. It is God's plan that his people be the hardest workers and the most loyal supporters of those they work for and live with. As you study the Bible's teaching on authority learn how to be a positive force for Christ in your world.

Your Attitude toward Authority. " . . . what is your attitude toward authority? Do you resent your foreman, your employer, or your company? How does that affect your attitude each day? Have you seen this resentment create circumstances that bring additional pressure upon you? God has ordained your relationship to that authority. When you rebel, you are really rebelling against God. This is true whether it is employer or government. If you have difficulty living in one authority structure, you will have difficulty in another. Some people have a history of problems with their supervisors. That is a sure sign of rebellion against God's established authority. Until your attitude is resolved to one which is biblical, you will never have real peace in your job."

Jerry and Mary White
Your Job—Survival or Satisfaction?
Zondervan Publishing House

BIBLE STUDY
Principles of Authority

Date of Studies_____

1. Read about the healing of the centurion's servant in Luke 7:2-10. What principles of authority did the centurion reveal?

_____
_____

2. Why did Jesus praise the man's faith? _____
_____
_____

3. Was Jesus under authority (John 5:30)? _____
_____
_____

4. How much authority did he possess (Matthew 28:18)?
_____
_____

5. What principles of authority can you extract from Luke 22:25-30? _____
_____
_____
_____

6. What responsibility goes with having parental authority (Numbers 14:18, 33)? _____
_____
_____

7. When you please God, what will happen (Proverbs 16:7)? How can this apply to an authority-submission situation?
_____
_____

BIBLE STUDY
Authority: God and Man

Date of Studies_____

1. What is the purpose of our being alive?

    a. Matthew 22:36, 37 _____

    b. 1 Peter 2:5, 9 _____

    c. Titus 2:14 _____

2. Why are we to submit to God (James 4:6, 7; 1 Peter 5:6)?
_____

3. What type of submission is involved in Romans 12:1, 2?
_____

4. Are there any benefits of submitting to God according to the above passages? _____

5. Describe the principles of discipline God uses on his children according to Hebrews 12:4-13. Why does he discipline us and what are the results?
_____

BIBLE STUDY
Authority: Government

Date of Studies_____

1. Who is in control of all governments (Proverbs 21:1; Romans 13:1)? _____
_____
_____
_____

2. Summarize every principle of authority contained in Romans 13:1-7 as it relates to governments. _____
_____
_____
_____
_____
_____
_____
_____
_____
_____

3. When is it right to disobey authority (Acts 4:18-20)?
_____
_____
_____
_____

4. Was Paul correct in reviling the high priest in Acts 23:1-5? _____
Why? _____
_____
_____

43

BIBLE STUDY
Authority: Husband and Wife

Date of Studies_____

Look up the following references and record each principle for husbands and wives. Put each principle in the appropriate column below. Ephesians 4:21-33; Colossians 3:18, 19; 1 Corinthians 7:1-16; 1 Peter 3:1-7.

Husbands	**Wives**

TAKE A LOOK AT YOURSELF
Check every statement that describes your present attitude toward the Bible and Bible study.   Date_____

- [ ] 1. I never seem to have the time to study. I prefer to read.
- [ ] 2. I just don't know how to study the Bible.
- [ ] 3. I'm a slow reader; it's too much work.
- [ ] 4. Why study? I wouldn't be able to understand it anyway.
- [ ] 5. I don't know where to begin. The Bible is so difficult to understand.
- [ ] 6. I don't believe everything the Bible teaches.
- [ ] 7. I study now and then.
- [ ] 8. I'm looking forward to learning how to study the Bible better.
- [ ] 9. I study the Bible regularly now.
- [ ] 10. _____

COMMITMENT NO. 4
"With the Lord's strength I commit myself to _____
_____
_____
_____
_____

_____   _____
(Disciple)   (Discipler)

_____   _____
(Date)   (Date)

RESOURCE SHEET
Obeying Parents

The Bible makes it plain that children are to obey their parents—but it goes much further. Here are some basic attitudes you are to have toward your parents:

- Reverence them (Leviticus 19:3).
- Obey them, be obedient (Ephesians 6:1; Colossians 3:20).
- Help support them if necessary (Matthew 15:3-7).
- Listen to them (Proverbs 23:22).
- Do not despise them (Proverbs 23:22).
- Make them glad (Proverbs 10:1).
- Honor them (Ephesians 6:2).
- Observe their teaching (Proverbs 6:20).
- Let their counsel go with you everywhere (Proverbs 6:21).

When you obey your parents, God will bless you. Here are some of the promises he gives. If you obey your parents:

- You will please the Lord (Colossians 3:20).
- You will be doing what is right (Ephesians 6:1).
- Things will go well with you (Ephesians 6:2, 3).
- You will live a longer life (Ephesians 6:3).
- Your son and grandson will have a greater desire to follow the Lord (Deuteronomy 5:16; 6:1, 2).
- You will receive guidance (Proverbs 6:22).
- You will be watched over (Proverbs 6:22).
- You will be talked to (Proverbs 6:22).
- You will be kept from the evil woman (Proverbs 6:24).

The basic intentions of most parents for their children are the following:

- They want their children to be happy.
- They want to feel they will still be needed.
- They want to see gratefulness in their children for what they have done.
- They want their children to have security.
- They want their children to be socially acceptable.

BIBLE STUDY
Authority: Employer-Employee

Date of Studies_____

1. Summarize how important it is for men to work.
(1 Thessalonians 4:11; 2 Thessalonians 3:6-12; 1 Timothy 5:8; Proverbs 6:6-11).

_____
_____
_____
_____
_____
_____

2. What principles are contained in Colossians 3:22-25, 1 Peter 2:18, and Ephesians 6:5-8 that you can use in responding to your employer?

_____
_____

3. What instruction can employers glean from Colossians 4:1 and Ephesians 6:9? _____

_____

4. What attitude does Jesus say we are to have in Matthew 20:25-28? _____

_____

5. What lessons can we learn from the ant (Proverbs 6:6-8)?

_____
_____
_____

BIBLE STUDY
Authority: Spiritual Leaders

Date of Studies _____

1. Summarize your responsibilities toward spiritual leadership in each of the following references:

   a. Hebrews 13:7; 1 Thessalonians 1:5, 6 _____
   _____
   _____

   b. 1 Thessalonians 5:12 _____
   _____
   _____

   c. 1 Thessalonians 5:13 _____
   _____
   _____

   d. Hebrews 13:17 _____
   _____
   _____

   e. Ephesians 5:21 _____
   _____
   _____

   f. Philippians 3:17 _____
   _____
   _____

2. Scripture contains many examples of one-on-one spiritual relationships. Think of Moses and Joshua, Elijah and Elisha, Barnabas and Paul, and later Paul and Timothy. Describe the qualities you desire in your spiritual leaders.

_____
_____
_____

48

MEMORY WORK SHEET

Scripture Reference _____ Date _____

1. Translation to be used: _____

2. Exact passage to be memorized: _____
_____
_____
_____
_____

3. When you're ready, review the passage above and quiz yourself by writing it here: _____
_____
_____
_____
_____
_____

4. Use this space for a second quiz of the passage: _____
_____
_____
_____
_____

5. Each time you review, list the date and check your score:

Review date	Perfect	Average	Poor
Review date_____	Perfect_____	Average_____	Poor_____
Review date_____	Perfect_____	Average_____	Poor_____
Review date_____	Perfect_____	Average_____	Poor_____
Review date_____	Perfect_____	Average_____	Poor_____
Review date_____	Perfect_____	Average_____	Poor_____
Review date_____	Perfect_____	Average_____	Poor_____

RESOURCE SHEET
Chain-of-Command
1. What is the purpose of authority?
    a. Things always seem to run smoothly when someone is in charge. If two people room together, one of them should have the "last say."
    b. Authority is also given to help each of us develop mature attitudes. Can you imagine how a child would turn out if he got his own way from the day of his birth? Obeying authority helps each of us learn right from wrong.
2. Why must we respect those in authority?
    a. No matter how poorly a person in authority behaves, never forget he is in command. God will bless us when we learn to obey those over us. We must learn to do what they tell us to, not to do what they do. Respect the position even if you can't respect the behavior of the person.
    b. God speaks through authority—whether or not it is Christian. God told Caesar Augustus to call a census—so that Joseph and Mary would travel to Bethlehem! God desires that you and I obey the parents, husbands, employers, governments, and spiritual leaders over us. When we do, he will show us his will.
3. What is the difference between chain-of-command and chain-of-counsel?
    a. Those who are directly over you or under you are in the chain-of-command. Baby-sitters, substitute teachers, and older brothers and sisters can all be delegated as our temporary authorities by those over us.
    b. Chain-of-counsel includes those people who have influence over us but no immediate authority: relatives, parents after marriage, former teachers, etc.
4. Which is the greatest authority?
   God is the ultimate authority. We must obey him before any earthly power. Peter and John refused to obey the priests (in Acts 4:19, 20) when they were told to stop preaching in Jesus' name. Make certain you always know which authority has a greater claim on your life.
5. How can you gain independence?
   There are some authorities which you will always be under. Other authorities such as parents, teachers, and employers will someday give up control over you. Don't demand to get your own way—earn independence. You earn independence by being loyal and obedient.

BOOK REPORT

Name of Book _____

Author _____ Publisher _____

Chapter(s) read _____

1. Chapter _____ summarized: _____
_____
_____
_____
_____

2. Chapter _____ summarized: _____
_____
_____
_____
_____

3. List important points you should remember: _____
_____
_____
_____
_____

4. What were the most impressive facts you learned? _____
_____
_____
_____
_____
_____

51

BOOK REPORT
Name of Book _____

Author _____ Publisher _____

Chapter(s) read _____

1. Chapter _____ summarized: _____
_____
_____
_____
_____

2. Chapter _____ summarized: _____
_____
_____
_____
_____

3. List important points you should remember: _____
_____
_____
_____
_____

4. What were the most impressive facts you learned? ___
_____
_____
_____
_____
_____

TAKE A LOOK AT YOURSELF

Date_____

1. In the second column below list the names of the immediate authority which you find directly over you. In the third column list any major problem you have with that authority.

	Immediate Authority	Major Problem
a. Government		
b. Husband		
c. Parents		
d. Employer		
e. Spiritual leaders		

2. List specific things that irritate you about each authority figure above:

_____
_____
_____

3. Check every statement that describes your attitude toward authority:

☐ 1. I cannot stand to take orders.

☐ 2. My parents still think of me as a child.

☐ 3. My employer doesn't know what he's doing. I sure wish I was the boss.

☐ 4. My husband is not a spiritual leader.

☐ 5. My wife is not submissive.

☐ 6. I enjoy making other people "look good."

☐ 7. I want to be known as a loyal person.

☐ 8. Nobody seems to see my potential as a leader.

☐ 9. I feel I'm making great strides toward becoming an obedient person.

RESOURCE SHEET

"We are all familiar with the proverb that 'the grass is greener on the other side of the fence.' We feel if we could just be somewhere else, things would be better. But they seldom are. Changing your circumstances will not generally solve your problems. Most problems are of our own making or are generated within ourselves. . . .

"Escaping from circumstances usually means escaping from reality. We do not want to face life as it really is. We live in the future hoping that things will change, or in the past wishing that things were as they used to be. To live full and meaningful lives, we must live in the present.

". . . God's objective is to use the pressures of real life to cause us to turn to Him. In John 16:33 Jesus promises constant pressure. 'In the world you have tribulation, but take courage; I have overcome the world.' The word <u>tribulation</u> is the same word used for pressing out the wine from the grapes. This verse could be translated 'in the world you have pressure.' We will never be able to escape those pressures, but we can have peace and fulfillment in the midst of them. Jesus says to 'take courage,' not to 'run away'; because He has overcome the world, we can successfully endure that stress."

Jerry and Mary White
<u>Your Job—Survival or Satisfaction</u>
Zondervan Publishing House

COMMITMENT NO. 4

"With the Lord's strength I commit myself to: _____

_____

_____

_____   _____

Disciple   Discipler

_____   _____

Date   Date

54

PLAN OF ATTACK
Authority

Date_____

Your discipler will share with you the necessary information to fill this page.

PLAN OF ATTACK
Authority

Date_____

Your discipler will share with you the necessary information to fill this page.

WHAT YOU'VE LEARNED

Date of Quiz_____

What have you learned in this section? This little quiz will give you an opportunity to see how much you've learned while studying the material in this chapter. Don't let this quiz worry you. Its purpose is not to give you a grade, but to show what you've learned. It will let you know in what areas you need work.

1. _____
2. _____
3. _____
4. _____
5. _____
6. _____
7. _____
8. _____
9. _____
10. _____
11. _____
12. _____
13. _____
14. _____
15. _____
16. _____
17. _____
18. _____

19. _____

20. _____

3
UNDERSTANDING YOURSELF

INTRODUCTION
Most Christians have a difficult time understanding why they are continually plagued by the same problems. Everyone has a list of basic temperament characteristics that makes him what he is. This section will help you study your own temperament strengths and weaknesses. It will guide you in overcoming persistent weaknesses and give you clues as to why you struggle continually in the same areas.

You're Born with It! "Temperament is the combination of inborn traits that subconsciously affects man's behavior. These traits are arranged genetically on the basis of nationality, race, sex, and other hereditary factors. These traits are passed on by the genes.

"Character is the real you. The Bible refers to it as 'the hidden man of the heart.' It is the result of your natural temperament modified by childhood training, education, and basic attitudes, beliefs, principles, and motivations. It is sometimes referred to as 'the soul' of man, which is made up of the mind, emotions, and will.

"Personality is the outward expression of ourselves, which may or may not be the same as our character, depending on how genuine we are. Often personality is a pleasing facade for an unpleasant or weak character. Many

part today on the basis of what they think a
...on should be, rather than what they really are. This is
a formula for mental and spiritual chaos. It is caused by
following the human formula for acceptable conduct. The
Bible tells us, 'Man looketh on the outward appearance,
and God looketh on the heart,' and 'Out of the heart
proceed the issues of life.' The place to change behavior is
inside man, not outside."

Tim LaHaye
<u>Spirit-Controlled Temperament</u>
Tyndale House Publishers

RESOURCE SHEET
Understanding your temperament is one of the most effective ways in which you can control your behavior. The purpose of this chapter is not to put a label on your behavior, but to discover your strengths and weaknesses. It doesn't matter what label is put on those temperament traits. What does matter is that you discover each natural tendency so the strengths can be developed and the weaknesses brought under control.

Many people have blind spots in their personalities. It is difficult for them to see themselves accurately. They may be totally unaware of what others see clearly. Or they may know their weaknesses but have no idea what strengths they possess.

The four theories of temperament are particularly valuable for such people with "tunnel vision." It is comforting to know that whatever weaknesses you may have, there is an excellent chance you also possess the corresponding strengths. All of us need to take a long look at our character and begin working on those areas which need repair.

COMMITMENT NO. 5
"It is my desire to _____
_____
_____
_____
_____

_____   _____
Disciple   Discipler

_____   _____
Date   Date

WORK SHEET
Character Analysis

Today's Date_____

Directions: Listed below are temperature strengths and weaknesses. Check off eight strengths and ten weaknesses that apply to you most.

Temperament Strengths

- ☐ Talkative
- ☐ Gifted
- ☐ Strong-willed
- ☐ Calm
- ☐ Outgoing
- ☐ Analytical
- ☐ Determined
- ☐ Easygoing
- ☐ Enthusiastic
- ☐ Sensitive
- ☐ Optimistic
- ☐ Warm
- ☐ Perfectionist
- ☐ Independent
- ☐ Efficient
- ☐ Personable
- ☐ Aesthetic
- ☐ Practical
- ☐ Conservative
- ☐ Friendly
- ☐ Idealistic
- ☐ Productive
- ☐ Dependable
- ☐ Compassionate
- ☐ Loyal
- ☐ Decisive
- ☐ Humorous
- ☐ Carefree
- ☐ Self-sacrificing
- ☐ Leader
- ☐ Diplomatic
- ☐ Enjoys life
- ☐ Confident

Temperament Weaknesses

- ☐ Weak-willed
- ☐ Self-centered
- ☐ Hot-tempered
- ☐ Unmotivated
- ☐ Unstable
- ☐ Depressive
- ☐ Cruel
- ☐ Lazy
- ☐ Undisciplined
- ☐ Negative
- ☐ Impulsive
- ☐ Slow
- ☐ Restless
- ☐ Self-sufficient
- ☐ Teaser
- ☐ Undependable
- ☐ Impractical
- ☐ Sarcastic
- ☐ Stubborn
- ☐ Egotistical
- ☐ Critical
- ☐ Domineering
- ☐ Indecisive
- ☐ Loud
- ☐ Revengeful
- ☐ Inconsiderate
- ☐ Stingy
- ☐ Exaggerates
- ☐ Introspective
- ☐ Unemotional
- ☐ Fearful
- ☐ Unsociable
- ☐ Rigid
- ☐ Crafty
- ☐ Spectator
- ☐ Proud
- ☐ Self-protective
- ☐ Selfish
- ☐ Theoretical

Your discipler will go over the strengths and weaknesses you have selected. He will help you design projects for each of the areas in which you are weak. He will also help you discover if you have strong natural tendencies toward any of the four major temperament types.

BOOK REPORT
Name of Book _____

Author _____ Publisher _____

Chapter(s) read _____

1. Chapter _____ summarized: _____
_____
_____
_____
_____
_____

2. Chapter _____ summarized: _____
_____
_____
_____
_____
_____

3. List important points you should remember: _____
_____
_____
_____
_____
_____

4. What were the most impressive facts you learned? _____
_____
_____
_____
_____
_____
_____

BOOK REPORT
Name of Book _____

Author _____ Publisher _____

Chapter(s) read _____

1. Chapter _____ summarized: _____
_____
_____
_____
_____
_____

2. Chapter _____ summarized: _____
_____
_____
_____
_____
_____

3. List important points you should remember: _____
_____
_____
_____
_____
_____

4. What were the most impressive facts you learned? ___
_____
_____
_____
_____
_____
_____

BIBLE STUDY
Character Weaknesses (M)

Directions: 1. With your discipler's help check each character weakness you possess. 2. Using a standard dictionary, define each weakness. 3. Indicate the opposite strength that needs to be developed. 4. Look up each reference and summarize its basic teaching.

☐ SELF-CENTERED (SELFISH) Date of Study _____

Defined: _____

Opposing strength: _____

Phil. 2:3, 4 _____

2 Pet. 2:10 _____

Gal. 5:26 _____

What can I apply to my own life? _____

☐ THEORETICAL Date of Study _____

Defined: _____

Opposing strength: _____

1 Tim. 1:4-7 _____

1 Tim. 6:3, 4 _____

Col. 2:8 _____

What can I apply to my own life? _____

BIBLE STUDY
Character Weaknesses (M)

☐ DEPRESSIVE   Date of Study _____

Defined: _____
_____

Opposing strength: _____

2 Cor. 7:6 _____

Psalm 139 _____
_____

Psalm 23 _____
_____

1 Thess. 5:17, 18; Eph. 5:20 _____
_____

Phil. 4:4-8 _____
_____

What can I apply to my own life? _____
_____

☐ REVENGEFUL   Date of Study _____

Defined: _____
_____

Opposing strength: _____

Matt. 5:38-42 _____
_____

Col. 3:8 _____
_____

Rom. 12:17-20 _____
_____

What can I apply to my own life? _____
_____

65

BIBLE STUDY
Character Weaknesses (M)

☐ UNSOCIABLE   Date of Study_____

Defined:_____

_____

Opposing strength:_____

Rom. 15:1, 2, 5 _____

_____

Rom. 12:10 _____

_____

Heb. 13:1-3 _____

_____

What can I apply to my own life? _____

_____

_____

☐ INTROSPECTIVE   Date of Study_____

Defined:_____

_____

Opposing strength:_____

1 John 3:21 _____

_____

Rom. 14:22 _____

_____

1 John 4:16-18 _____

_____

What can I apply to my own life? _____

_____

_____

_____

BIBLE STUDY
Character Weaknesses (M)

☐ CRITICAL   Date of Study_____

Defined:_____
_____

Opposing strength:_____
1 Cor. 13:7_____
_____

Gal. 5:26 _____
_____

Luke 18:9-14 _____
_____
_____

What can I apply to my own life? _____
_____
_____

☐ NEGATIVE   Date of Study_____

Defined:_____
_____

Opposing strength:_____
Prov. 22:13 _____
_____

Phil. 4:8_____
_____

1 Pet. 5:7 _____
_____

What can I apply to my own life? _____
_____
_____

BIBLE STUDY
Character Weaknesses (P)

☐ TEASER   Date of Study_____

Defined:_____

Opposing strength:_____

Prov. 26:18, 19 _____

Eph. 5:4_____

What can I apply to my own life? _____

☐ INDECISIVE   Date of Study_____

Defined:_____

Opposing strength:_____

Prov. 3:5, 6 _____

Eph. 4:14 _____

1 Cor. 14:40 _____

What can I apply to my own life? _____

BIBLE STUDY
Character Weaknesses (P)

☐ UNMOTIVATED   Date of Study_____

Defined:_____

_____

Opposing strength:_____

Prov. 6:9-11 _____

_____

_____

Prov. 26:14, 15 _____

_____

What can I apply to my own life? _____

_____

☐ LAZY/SLOW   Date of Study_____

Defined:_____

_____

Opposing strength:_____

Prov. 24:30-34_____

_____

Prov. 6:6-8 _____

_____

Prov. 13:4_____

_____

Rom. 12:11 _____

_____

What can I apply to my own life? _____

_____

_____

BIBLE STUDY
Character Weaknesses (P)

☐ STINGY   Date of Study_____
Defined:_____
Opposing strength:_____
Rom. 12:8_____
_____

2 Cor. 9:6-11_____
_____

Prov. 22:9_____
_____

Prov. 11:25_____
_____

Luke 6:38_____
_____

What can I apply to my own life?_____
_____

☐ FEARFUL   Date of Study_____
Defined:_____
Opposing strength:_____
Rom. 8:15, 31-39_____
_____

2 Tim. 1:7_____
_____

1 John 4:16-18_____
_____

What can I apply to my own life?_____
_____
_____

70

BIBLE STUDY
Character Weaknesses (P/S)

☐ STUBBORN (P)   Date of Study _____

Defined: _____

Opposing strength: _____

Prov. 29:1 _____

_____

1 Sam. 15:23 _____

_____

Judges 2:19 _____

_____

Psalm 78:8 _____

_____

What can I apply to my own life? _____

_____

_____

☐ EMOTIONALLY UNSTABLE (S)   Date of Study _____

Defined: _____

_____

Opposing strength: _____

Prov. 25:26 _____

_____

Prov. 24:21 _____

_____

Rom. 12:21 _____

_____

What can I apply to my own life? _____

_____

_____

BIBLE STUDY
Character Weaknesses (S)

☐ IMPULSIVE   Date of Study _____

Defined: _____

Opposing strength: _____

Luke 14:28-33 _____

_____

Prov. 29:20 _____

_____

What can I apply to my own life? _____

_____

_____

☐ UNDISCIPLINED   Date of Study _____

Defined: _____

_____

Opposing strength: _____

1 Tim. 4:7, 8 _____

_____

Heb. 12:11 _____

_____

1 Cor. 9:24-27 _____

_____

2 Tim. 2:4 _____

_____

2 Cor. 10:4, 5 _____

_____

What can I apply to my own life? _____

_____

_____

BIBLE STUDY
Character Weaknesses (S)

☐ WEAK-WILLED   Date of Study_____

Defined:_____
_____

Opposing strength:_____

1 Pet. 4:1-3 _____
_____

1 Tim. 5:6 _____
_____

Gal. 5:16, 17, 24 _____
_____

2 Pet. 2:13, 14 _____
_____

What can I apply to my own life? _____
_____
_____

☐ EGOTISTICAL   Date of Study_____

Defined:_____
Opposing strength:_____

Prov. 29:23 _____
_____

Prov. 26:12 _____
_____

2 Cor. 10:12 _____
_____

What can I apply to my own life? _____
_____
_____

73

BIBLE STUDY
Character Weaknesses (S)

☐ UNDEPENDABLE   Date of Study_____

Defined:_____

Opposing strength:_____

Prov. 25:19 _____

_____

Prov. 20:6 _____

_____

Rom. 1:31 _____

_____

Gal. 5:22 _____

_____

What can I apply to my own life? _____

_____

☐ EXAGGERATES   Date of Study_____

Defined:_____

_____

Opposing strength:_____

Prov. 25:14 _____

_____

Prov. 25:27 _____

_____

Prov. 27:2 _____

_____

What can I apply to my own life? _____

_____

_____

BIBLE STUDY
Character Weaknesses (C)

☐ HOT-TEMPERED Date of Study _____

Defined: _____
_____

Opposing strength: _____

Prov. 22:24, 25 _____
_____

Prov. 29:11, 22 _____
_____

Eph. 4:26 _____
_____

What can I apply to my own life? _____
_____
_____

☐ SELF-SUFFICIENT Date of Study _____

Defined: _____
_____

Opposing strength: _____

Luke 12:16-20 _____
_____
_____

Prov. 3:5, 6 _____
_____

Jer. 9:23, 24 _____
_____

What can I apply to my own life? _____
_____
_____

BIBLE STUDY
Character Weaknesses (C)

☐ PROUD   Date of Study_____
Defined:_____
Opposing strength:_____
Prov. 16:5_____
_____
Jer. 50:31, 32 _____
_____
_____
1 Pet. 5:5 _____
_____
What can I apply to my own life? _____
_____
_____

☐ INCONSIDERATE   Date of Study_____
Defined:_____
_____
Opposing strength:_____
Rom. 12:10 _____
_____
1 Cor. 13:5_____
_____
Phil. 2:3, 4_____
_____
_____
What can I apply to my own life? _____
_____
_____

BIBLE STUDY
Character Weaknesses (C)

☐ CRUEL   Date of Study_____

Defined:_____

Opposing strength:_____

Prov. 6:17 _____
_____

Prov. 1:11-19 _____
_____

Prov. 28:17 _____
_____

What can I apply to my own life? _____
_____
_____

☐ SARCASTIC   Date of Study_____

Defined:_____
_____

Opposing strength:_____

Eph. 5:4_____
_____

Eph. 4:29 _____
_____

Col. 3:8 _____
_____

James 3:10 _____
_____

What can I apply to my own life? _____
_____
_____

BOOK REPORT
Name of Book _____

Author _____ Publisher _____

Chapter(s) read _____

1. Chapter _____ summarized: _____
_____
_____
_____
_____
_____

2. Chapter _____ summarized: _____
_____
_____
_____
_____
_____

3. List important points you should remember: _____
_____
_____
_____
_____
_____

4. What were the most impressive facts you learned? _____
_____
_____
_____
_____
_____
_____

78

MEMORY WORK SHEET

Scripture Reference _____ Date _____

1. Translation to be used: _____
2. Exact passage to be memorized: _____
   _____
   _____
   _____

3. When you're ready, review the passage above and quiz yourself by writing it here: _____
   _____
   _____
   _____
   _____
   _____

4. Use this space for a second quiz of the passage: _____
   _____
   _____
   _____
   _____
   _____

5. Each time you review, list the date and check your score:

Review date _____ Perfect _____ Average _____ Poor _____
Review date _____ Perfect _____ Average _____ Poor _____
Review date _____ Perfect _____ Average _____ Poor _____
Review date _____ Perfect _____ Average _____ Poor _____
Review date _____ Perfect _____ Average _____ Poor _____
Review date _____ Perfect _____ Average _____ Poor _____

BIBLE STUDY
Biography

Your discipler will introduce the material to you for one or two Bible biography studies. These studies will center upon the visible temperament strengths and weaknesses of the Bible character you select.

Date_____ Name of Character_____

1. Basic background passages to read: _____
   _____
   _____

2. Summarize the character's life story: _____
   _____
   _____
   _____
   _____
   _____
   _____
   _____

3. References which reveal temperament weaknesses:
   _____
   _____

4. Summarize his weaknesses: _____
   _____
   _____
   _____
   _____
   _____
   _____
   _____

BIBLE STUDY
Biography

Date_____ Name of Character_____

5. References which reveal temperament strengths:_____
_____
_____

6. Summarize his strengths: _____
_____
_____
_____
_____
_____
_____

7. References which reveal God's transforming power in his life: _____
_____

8. Summarize the transformation which God brought about:
_____
_____
_____
_____
_____

9. In what ways are you like this character (both strengths and weaknesses)? _____
_____
_____
_____

PLAN OF ATTACK
Character Weaknesses

Date_____

On the next few pages list the major weaknesses over which you desire to gain great control. Your discipler will work out projects for each temperament difficulty.

1. WEAKNESS: _____

_____

_____

_____

_____

_____

_____

_____

_____

_____

2. WEAKNESS: _____

_____

_____

_____

_____

_____

_____

_____

_____

_____

_____

PLAN OF ATTACK
Character Weaknesses

Date_____

3. WEAKNESS: _____
_____
_____
_____
_____
_____
_____
_____

4. WEAKNESS: _____
_____
_____
_____
_____
_____
_____

5. WEAKNESS: _____
_____
_____
_____
_____
_____
_____

83

PLAN OF ATTACK
Positive Character Qualities

Date_____

Now list some of the strengths you would like to develop more fully.

1. STRENGTH: _____
_____
_____
_____

2. STRENGTH: _____
_____
_____
_____

3. STRENGTH: _____
_____
_____
_____

4. STRENGTH: _____
_____
_____
_____

5. STRENGTH: _____
_____
_____
_____

84

WHAT YOU'VE LEARNED

Date of Quiz_____

What have you learned in this section? This little quiz will give you an opportunity to see how much you've learned while studying the material in this chapter. Don't let this quiz worry you. Its purpose is not to give you a grade, but to show what you've learned. It will let you know in what areas you need work.

1. _____
2. _____
3. _____
4. _____
5. _____
6. _____
7. _____
8. _____
9. _____
10. _____
11. _____
12. _____
13. _____
14. _____
15. _____
16. _____
17. _____
18. _____
_____
19. _____
_____
20. _____
_____

KNOWING GOD'S WILL

INTRODUCTION
"If only I knew what God's will was, I would obey it."
Have you ever made that statement? Knowing God's will seems to be one of the hardest things for us to do.

This section will give you new insights into finding God's will for your life. If you learn and practice the biblical principles contained here, you will begin to know God's will—or at least how to find it when you're in doubt.

Taking the Yoke. "Many have made shipwreck of their lives by failing to seek the will of God right from their youth. It is indeed 'good for a man that he bear the yoke in his youth' (Lamentations 3:27). In Matthew 11:28-30, Jesus invites us to take his yoke upon us. What does it mean to take the yoke? In the villages of India, the farmers plow their fields with pairs of oxen. The oxen are kept together by a yoke upon their necks. When a new ox is to be trained to plow, it is yoked together with an experienced ox. The new one is thus compelled to walk in the <u>same direction</u> and at the <u>same speed</u> as the older ox.

"This is what it means to take the yoke of Jesus upon us. We shall have to walk with Jesus in the path that pleases Him, never rushing ahead to do anything without His leading, nor lagging behind when He calls to some new step of obedience. Few understand this meaning of the yoke. Fewer still are willing to accept it. The ox is forced by its owner to take the yoke upon its neck. But Jesus <u>invites</u> us. There is no compulsion here. How foolish we are to reject this invitation!"

Zac Poonen
<u>Where Do I Go from Here?</u>
Tyndale House Publishers

TAKE A LOOK AT YOURSELF

Date_____

Check every statement that describes where you are in relation to God's will.

- [ ] 1. Sometimes I know I'm in the center of God's will.
- [ ] 2. I'm never sure I'm in his will.
- [ ] 3. God has blessed me, I must be in his will.
- [ ] 4. God speaks very plainly to me.
- [ ] 5. I'm not really sure if God speaks to me or if I just get impulses.
- [ ] 6. I'm afraid of knowing God's will. He might send me somewhere like Africa!
- [ ] 7. There are some areas of my life in which I already know what I want. I don't want to know his will.
- [ ] 8. _____

COMMITMENT NO. 6
"With the Lord's strength I commit myself to _____
_____
_____
_____

_____   _____
Disciple   Discipler

_____   _____
Date   Date

BIBLE STUDY
What Is God's Will?

Date of Studies_____

1. What do you think is God's basic will? _____
_____
_____

2. What do Matthew 7:21 and 1 John 2:17 tell you? _____
_____
_____
_____

3. The following references specifically say "this is God's will." Summarize his will in each case.

   a. John 6:40 _____
   _____
   _____

   b. 1 Thessalonians 4:3_____
   _____
   _____

   c. 1 Thessalonians 5:18 _____
   _____
   _____

   d. 1 Peter 2:15 _____
   _____
   _____

4. How important was the Father's will to Jesus (John 4:34; 5:30)?_____
_____
_____
_____

BIBLE STUDY
Hunger for God's Will

Date of Studies_____

1. How much do you want God's will in your life? Be honest.

_____
_____
_____

2. How much did David want God's will in his life (Psalm 40:8)? _____

_____
_____

3. How are we to approach God (Jeremiah 29:13)? _____

_____
_____

4. Why do you think we are to come this way?_____

_____

5. Has God set you free from sin so that you can do his will (1 Peter 4:1, 2)? _____

_____

6. Most Christians already know what they want to do before they ask God for guidance. They are actually asking for his stamp of approval on their decisions. Does this happen to you? If it does, give an example.

_____
_____
_____
_____
_____

BOOK REPORT

Name of Book _____

Author _____ Publisher _____

Chapter(s) read _____

1. Chapter _____ summarized: _____
_____
_____
_____
_____
_____

2. Chapter _____ summarized: _____
_____
_____
_____
_____
_____

3. List important points you should remember: _____
_____
_____
_____
_____
_____

4. What were the most impressive facts you learned? ____
_____
_____
_____
_____
_____
_____

91

BIBLE STUDY
Paying the Price

Date of Studies_____

1. You can prove what the good and acceptable and perfect will of God is by doing what (Romans 12:1, 2)?_____
_____
_____
_____

2. In practical terms, how can you do the above? _____
_____
_____
_____

3. What are you <u>not</u> to do according to Proverbs 3:5, 6?
_____
_____
_____

4. What are you to do according to the same passage?
_____
_____

5. Jesus said we could do nothing without him (John 15:5). What did he mean?_____
_____
_____
_____

6. Do you find yourself justifying your own actions (Proverbs 16:2; 21:2)? _____
_____
_____
_____

BIBLE STUDY
Obtaining Wise Counsel

Date of Studies _____

1. Look up each of the following references and summarize what they tell you about obtaining wise counsel.

   a. Proverbs 11:14 _____

   b. Proverbs 12:15 _____

   c. Proverbs 15:22 _____

   d. Proverbs 19:20, 21 _____

   e. Proverbs 21:30 _____

2. Whom can you go to for counsel? _____

3. Do you ever ask your parents for counsel (Prov. 6:20-24)? _____

4. How can you determine if the counsel you are receiving is from God? _____

93

BOOK REPORT
Name of Book _____

Author _____ Publisher _____

Chapter(s) read _____

1. Chapter _____ summarized: _____
_____
_____
_____
_____
_____

2. Chapter _____ summarized: _____
_____
_____
_____
_____
_____

3. List important points you should remember: _____
_____
_____
_____
_____
_____

4. What were the most impressive facts you learned? __
_____
_____
_____
_____
_____
_____

BIBLE STUDY
Finding God's Will

Date of Studies _____

1. Look up the following verses and glean any principles of conduct that will help you determine God's will.

   a. Psalm 25:3, 5, 21; 37:7 _____
   _____
   _____

   b. Psalm 37:5 _____
   _____

   c. 2 Timothy 3:16, 17 _____
   _____
   _____

   d. Colossians 3:15 _____
   _____

   e. Colossians 3:17, 23 _____
   _____
   _____

   f. Philippians 4:6, 7 _____
   _____

   g. Romans 8:14 _____
   _____

2. Summarize the things the Word tells you to do so you can know God's will. (Use the last five Bible study pages.) _____
_____
_____
_____
_____
_____

95

MEMORY WORK SHEET

Scripture Reference _____ Date _____

1. Translation to be used: _____

2. Exact passage to be memorized: _____
   _____
   _____
   _____
   _____

3. When you're ready, review the passage above and quiz yourself by writing it here: _____
   _____
   _____
   _____
   _____
   _____

4. Use this space for a second quiz of the passage: _____
   _____
   _____
   _____
   _____
   _____

5. Each time you review, list the date and check your score:

Review date_____ Perfect_____ Average_____ Poor_____
Review date_____ Perfect_____ Average_____ Poor_____
Review date_____ Perfect_____ Average_____ Poor_____
Review date_____ Perfect_____ Average_____ Poor_____
Review date_____ Perfect_____ Average_____ Poor_____
Review date_____ Perfect_____ Average_____ Poor_____

BOOK REPORT
Name of Book _____

Author _____ Publisher _____

Chapter(s) read _____

1. Chapter _____ summarized: _____
_____
_____
_____
_____
_____

2. Chapter _____ summarized: _____
_____
_____
_____
_____

3. List important points you should remember: _____
_____
_____
_____
_____

4. What were the most impressive facts you learned? ___
_____
_____
_____
_____
_____
_____

97

PLAN OF ATTACK
God's Will

Date_____

Your discipler will share with you the information necessary to fill this page.

1._____

_____

_____

_____

2._____

_____

_____

_____

_____

3._____

_____

_____

_____

4._____

_____

_____

_____

_____

5._____

_____

_____

_____

_____

WORK SHEET
The Will of God

Date of Studies_____

1. Write down the details of a decision you are pondering, or some situation about which you wish to learn God's will.

_____

_____

_____

2. Does the Word of God have anything to say on this subject?_____ If so, what?_____

_____

_____

_____

3. List the counsel you have received (and from what sources). _____

_____

_____

4. List the pros and cons of a possible decision.

Pros	**Cons**

5. Do you have peace? _____

6. Have you talked to God in prayer? Have you waited on him? _____

_____

7. Your final decision: _____

WORK SHEET
The Will of God

Date of Studies_____

1. Write down the details of a decision you are pondering, or some situation about which you wish to learn God's will.

_____
_____
_____

2. Does the Word of God have anything to say on this subject?_____ If so, what?_____

_____
_____

3. List the counsel you have received (and from what sources). _____

_____
_____

4. List the pros and cons of a possible decision.

Pros	**Cons**

5. Do you have peace? _____

6. Have you talked to God in prayer? Have you waited on him? _____

_____

7. Your final decision: _____

WHAT YOU'VE LEARNED

Date of Quiz_____

What have you learned in this section? This little quiz will give you an opportunity to see how much you've learned while studying the material in this chapter. Don't let this quiz worry you. Its purpose is not to give you a grade, but to show what you've learned. It will let you know in what areas you need work.

1. _____
2. _____
3. _____
4. _____
5. _____
6. _____
7. _____
8. _____
9. _____
10. _____
11. _____
12. _____
13. _____
14. _____
15. _____
16. _____
17. _____
18. _____
_____
19. _____
_____
20. _____
_____

5
LEARNING TO LOVE

INTRODUCTION
When talking about living the Christian life, it is easy to think of Christianity only in terms of our own interests. But Christianity is a relationship with Christ in which we let him reach out to others through our personalities. Loving others does not come easily, because we are all naturally selfish people. In this section you will begin to work on your relationships with others and learn to love more freely and more fully.

The Oxygen of the Kingdom. "For many years I thought of love as one of the virtues of the Christian life. In my sermons I told people it was one of the most important things.

"Then I began to experience real love. And I found that it is not one of the virtues of the Christian life—love is the Christian life. It is not one of the most important things—it is the one thing. . . .

"It is the oxygen; there is no life without it. Love is the only eternal element. The other tremendous elements —gifts, tongues, prophecies, wisdom, knowledge, Bible reading, prayer—will all come to an end. The only thing that will go through death and into the eternal is love. . . .

"When love is generated from the inside, it solves all kinds of problems. The fruit of the Spirit is love—as well as joy, peace, patience, kindness, goodness, faithfulness, gentleness, and self-control (Galatians 5:22, 23). Why do we preach so much? Because we want to build love and these other things in the Christians. But if love were growing as it should, we wouldn't need so many sermons. Love is not one of the elements of the Christian life—it is <u>the</u> element. Love is the life itself.

"Some people fool themselves by seeking the Spirit's gifts instead of His fruit. Even though we appreciate the gifts, we must be careful where we put the emphasis. Jesus never said, 'You will know them by their gifts.' He said, 'You will know them by their fruits' (Matthew 7:20).

". . . A person may be excused if he doesn't have gifts, but there is no excuse for not having fruit. If we say to the apple tree, 'Why don't you have a nice ring on you?' the tree could say, 'Excuse me, but no one has put a ring on me.' But the tree cannot get away without having apples on it, because apples are the result of a normal apple tree.

"So we cannot excuse ourselves for not having love. If we are full of the Spirit, the natural thing is for us to be loving."

Juan Carlos Ortiz
<u>Disciple</u>
<u>Creation</u> House

103

BIBLE STUDY
Love Principles

Date of Studies_____

1. What was the commandment Christ gave in John 13:34, 35? _____
_____
_____

2. Why do you think a commandment was necessary? _____
_____
_____

3. What kind of love was Jesus suggesting? _____
_____

4. What does 1 John 4:7, 8 indicate that a Christian's love proves? _____
_____
_____

5. What is the greatest commandment (Matthew 22:36-38)? _____
_____

6. What is the second commandment (Matthew 22:39, 40)? _____
_____
_____

7. Why is love so important? _____
_____
_____

BIBLE STUDY
The Love Chapter

Date of Studies_____

Read 1 Corinthians 13 and list everything love is or that it is not in the column marked "principles" below.

	Principles	**Application**
1.		
2.		
3.		
4.		
5.		
6.		
7.		
8.		
9.		
10.		
11.		
12.		
13.		
14.		
15.		
16.		
17.		
18.		
19.		
20.		

In the application column indicate whether or not you are presently loving correctly according to each of the positive principles you have written down above. Indicate with the words "good," "average," or "poor" for your performance with each principle.

BIBLE STUDY
Love Your Enemy

Date of Studies_____

1. Read Matthew 5:43-48. What are we commanded to do?
_____
_____

Why? _____
_____
_____
_____

2. What practical ways does Jesus give to fulfill this in Matthew 5:38-42? _____
_____
_____
_____
_____

3. What practical ways does Jesus give to fulfill this type of love in Matthew 5:21-26?_____
_____
_____
_____
_____
_____

4. What practical way does Jesus give to fulfill this type of love in Matthew 5:10, 16? _____
_____
_____
_____
_____

BIBLE STUDY
Love Your Neighbor

Date of Studies_____

1. Read Luke 10:25-37. What was Jesus' answer to the question the lawyer asked?_____
_____
_____

2. What type of person is your neighbor, according to this passage? _____
_____
_____

3. Who is your neighbor then? Be specific. _____
_____
_____
_____

4. Sum up how you are to treat your neighbor according to each of the following passages:

   a. Romans 13:9, 10 _____
_____
_____

   b. Romans 15:1, 2_____
_____
_____

   c. Galatians 5:13, 14_____
_____
_____

   d. Ephesians 4:25_____
_____
_____

107

BOOK REPORT
Name of Book _____

Author _____ Publisher _____

Chapter(s) read _____

1. Chapter _____ summarized: _____
_____
_____
_____
_____
_____

2. Chapter _____ summarized: _____
_____
_____
_____
_____
_____

3. List important points you should remember: _____
_____
_____
_____
_____
_____

4. What were the most impressive facts you learned? _____
_____
_____
_____
_____
_____
_____

BOOK REPORT
Name of Book _____

Author _____ Publisher _____

Chapter(s) read _____

1. Chapter _____ summarized: _____
   _____
   _____
   _____
   _____
   _____

2. Chapter _____ summarized: _____
   _____
   _____
   _____
   _____
   _____

3. List important points you should remember: _____
   _____
   _____
   _____
   _____
   _____

4. What were the most impressive facts you learned?____
   _____
   _____
   _____
   _____
   _____
   _____

109

TAKE A LOOK AT YOURSELF

Date_____

1. Check every statement below that describes how you feel about other people.

- ☐ a. I like people.
- ☐ b. People seem to like me.
- ☐ c. It's fun to do things for other people.
- ☐ d. It's difficult for me to do things for others.
- ☐ e. I'm a shy person. I get embarrassed easily.
- ☐ f. People don't like to have me around.
- ☐ g. It's really a chore for me to meet people.
- ☐ h. I really have difficulty expressing love for others.
- ☐ i. It's easy for me to tell my friends how much I care.

2. List the names of your close friends. _____
_____
_____
_____

3. List the names of people you would consider as your "neighbors." _____
_____
_____
_____
_____

4. List the names of your enemies (former friends—people who don't like you). _____
_____
_____
_____
_____

TAKE A LOOK AT YOURSELF

5. In what way should your attitude toward others be changed? _____
_____
_____
_____
_____

6. In what ways should your actions toward others be changed? _____
_____
_____
_____
_____

COMMITMENT NO. 7
"With the Lord's strength I commit myself to _____
_____
_____
_____
_____
_____

_____   _____
Disciple   Discipler

_____   _____
Date   Date

111

BOOK REPORT
Name of Book _____

Author _____ Publisher _____

Chapter(s) read _____

1. Chapter _____ summarized: _____
_____
_____
_____
_____

2. Chapter _____ summarized: _____
_____
_____
_____
_____

3. List important points you should remember: _____
_____
_____
_____
_____

4. What were the most impressive facts you learned?___
_____
_____
_____
_____
_____

PLAN OF ATTACK
Brotherly Love

Date_____

PLAN OF ATTACK
The Disadvantaged

Date_____

114

WHAT YOU'VE LEARNED

Date of Quiz_____

What have you learned in this section? This little quiz will give you an opportunity to see how much you've learned while studying the material in this chapter. Don't let this quiz worry you. Its purpose is not to give you a grade, but to show what you've learned. It will let you know in what areas you need work.

1. _____
2. _____
3. _____
4. _____
5. _____
6. _____
7. _____
8. _____
9. _____
10. _____
11. _____
12. _____
13. _____
14. _____
15. _____
16. _____
17. _____
18. _____
_____
19. _____
_____
20. _____
_____

6
SHARING YOUR FAITH

INTRODUCTION
Personal evangelism is essential to discipleship. Whenever you find a disciple of Jesus, you will find a man or woman who is committed to the task of sharing his or her faith with the world. There can be no other way.

A Strategy for World Liberation. "Nineteen centuries have come and gone since Jesus told his followers to go, but that command still stands. The task of reaching the world is not finished. The Master said the gospel must be preached 'in the whole world . . . to all nations,' before the end would come.

"When Jesus told the disciples they were going to evangelize the world, he did not say, 'Only the men will go,' or 'Only those of you who like to talk will do this work.' No, Jesus didn't say that, because everyone was to go. Everyone was to become involved.

"As disciples of Jesus Christ we should be actively sharing the fact that Jesus is alive! The first century disciples were, initially, just as unqualified to start a world liberation movement as we may be today.

"Jesus said, 'Follow me, and I will make you fishers of men.' If we're not fishing for men, there's a good chance we're not following either. Just as he trained the disciples to reach their world, the Master wants to train us to reach our world.

"God knows our limitations far better than we do. Because he created us, he knows exactly what our abilities are. God wants us to reach our world, and he'll give us all the tools necessary to do that job, if we will only let him.

"A witness is someone who has seen something. In the book of Acts the disciples gave witness again and again to what they had seen—the resurrection of Jesus Christ. They shared it because they had had a personal experience with the risen Lord.

"You are to witness what you have experienced—not only that Jesus is alive—but that he is living in your heart. Witnessing is really not 'what' you know; it is 'who' you know. The better you know Jesus, the easier you will find it to share him with others."

John C. Souter
<u>Jesus the Liberator</u>
Tyndale House Publishers

117

TAKE A LOOK AT YOURSELF

Date_____

Check every statement that describes your present attitude about sharing your faith.

- [ ] 1. I want to share my faith.
- [ ] 2. The thought of witnessing really scares me.
- [ ] 3. I would really rather not share my faith.
- [ ] 4. I'm afraid I'm just no good at witnessing.
- [ ] 5. Evangelism is certainly not my spiritual gift.
- [ ] 6. I don't know how to witness, but I'm anxious to learn.
- [ ] 7. I enjoy sharing my faith and God has blessed my witnessing.
- [ ] 8. Witnessing comes easy to me.
- [ ] 9. I'm anxious to lead someone to the Lord.
- [ ] 10. _____

_____

_____

COMMITMENT NO. 8

"With the Lord's strength I commit myself to: _____

_____

_____

_____

_____   _____
(Disciple)   (Discipler)

_____   _____
(Date)   (Date)

118

BIBLE STUDY
Why Share Your Faith?

Date of Studies_____

1. Summarize each of the following commands of Christ:

    Matthew 5:14-16 _____
    _____
    _____

    Matthew 28:19, 20 _____
    _____
    _____

    John 14:12 _____
    _____

    John 15:26, 27 _____
    _____
    _____

    Acts 1:8 _____
    _____
    _____

2. Summarize the commands given by other New Testament writers concerning your personal witness.

    Colossians 4:3-6 _____
    _____
    _____

    2 Timothy 2:2 _____
    _____
    _____

    1 Peter 3:15 _____
    _____
    _____

119

BIBLE STUDY
What Is a Witness?

Date of Studies _____

1. Write down the definition of a "witness" from a standard dictionary. _____
_____
_____

2. What event were the disciples witnesses of in each of the following verses?

   Acts 1:22 _____
   Acts 2:32 _____
   Acts 3:15 _____
   Acts 4:33 _____

3. What then, in your opinion, does it mean to be a Christian witness? _____
_____
_____
_____

4. What "methods" did the Apostle Paul use in his ministry according to 1 Corinthians 9:19-23? _____
_____
_____
_____

5. Although Paul used whatever approach necessary to bring men to Christ, did he use dishonest methods? (See 1 Thessalonians 2:1-12.)

_____
_____
_____
_____

120

BOOK REPORT
Name of Book _____

Author _____ Publisher _____

Chapter(s) read _____

1. Chapter _____ summarized: _____
_____
_____
_____
_____

2. Chapter _____ summarized: _____
_____
_____
_____
_____

3. List important points you should remember: _____
_____
_____
_____
_____

4. What were the most impressive facts you learned? ____
_____
_____
_____
_____
_____

121

PLAN OF ATTACK
How to Witness

Date_____

WORK SHEET
Selecting a Plan of Salvation

Date of Studies_____

With your discipler's help, record the principles and verse references of several popular plans of salvation below. When you have copied several, decide which one best suits your personality and witnessing needs.

_____
_____
_____
_____
_____
_____
_____
_____
_____
_____
_____
_____
_____
_____
_____
_____
_____
_____
_____
_____
_____
_____
_____
_____

123

MEMORY WORK SHEET

Date You Begin Memorizing_____

1. So that you will never be at a loss for words when you witness, copy down a plan of salvation below and the references under each point.

_____
_____
_____
_____
_____
_____
_____

2. Memorize each salvation principle and reference. (You should have a good idea what each verse says.)
3. When you're ready, review the above plan and write it below:

_____
_____
_____
_____
_____

4. Review the references and principles daily until they are yours. Once you have them memorized, review them every week or two. Record your progress here:

Review date_____Perfect_____Average_____Poor_____
Review date_____Perfect_____Average_____Poor_____
Review date_____Perfect_____Average_____Poor_____
Review date_____Perfect_____Average_____Poor_____
Review date_____Perfect_____Average_____Poor_____
Review date_____Perfect_____Average_____Poor_____

RESOURCE SHEET
The Personal Testimony
Why Use Your Testimony?

The early Christian church used the testimony frequently because it was one of the most effective methods of presenting the gospel. Compare Paul's two testimonies in chapters 22 and 26 with his actual conversion in Acts 9. See how he revealed different things for different audiences?

When a Christian shares his own need and how Christ met it, a non-Christian is likely to say to himself, "That sounds like me. I need God just like he did." A testimony keeps you from preaching and helps you simply present Christ.

Do you feel you haven't got a testimony? Then you are looking at yourself and not at Christ. There is no such thing as an uninteresting testimony, because each reveals the power of God to save us from sin.

Knowing Christ should be the most important thing that has ever happened to you. If it is, you will want others to know. Your personal testimony is an effective way of communicating the fact that Jesus is alive. He is real because he is alive in your life—right now!

How to Present Your Testimony

A testimony should always be organized. It may be ad-libbed to keep it fresh, but for it to be effective, it should have a logical sequence and a natural conclusion. You will find that the Holy Spirit will use you best when your thoughts are organized. Use this basic outline:

1. Before—What were you like before becoming a Christian? Your feelings, your emptiness, and your problems should be shared here. Don't dwell on all your past sins if they have been many (Acts 26:9-11).

2. How—Explain the way in which you received Christ. Go into detail. Be certain you make it plain how you went about receiving Christ (Acts 26:12-18).

3. After—Give tangible examples of what Jesus has done for you since you became a Christian (Acts 26:19-22). Be positive, smile, and share a verse which explains what has happened in your life. Above all, pray God will use your words to reach the hearts of those who hear your story.

125

WORK SHEET
The Personal Testimony

Date_____

1._____

_____
_____
_____
_____
_____
_____
_____
_____

2._____

_____
_____
_____
_____
_____
_____
_____

3._____

_____
_____
_____
_____
_____
_____
_____

BIBLE STUDY
Spirit-Controlled Witnessing

Date of Studies_____

1. Examine how Philip was led by the Holy Spirit in his witnessing in Acts 8. Summarize each account.

vv. 5-8 _____

v. 26 _____

v. 29 _____

2. What light does Romans 8:14 throw on the above?_____
_____
_____
_____

3. What will the Holy Spirit help us do (John 15:26, 27; Acts 1:8)? _____
_____
_____

4. How do you feel the Spirit will help you accomplish the above task? _____
_____

5. How does the Holy Spirit prepare the hearts of men according to John 16:8-11?_____
_____

6. Can a man come to Christ if his heart is not prepared (John 6:44, 65)? _____
_____
_____

WHAT YOU'VE LEARNED

Date of Quiz _____

What have you learned in this section? This little quiz will give you an opportunity to see how much you've learned while studying the material in this chapter. Don't let this quiz worry you. Its purpose is not to give you a grade, but to show what you've learned. It will let you know in what areas you need work.

1. _____
2. _____
3. _____
4. _____
5. _____
6. _____
7. _____
8. _____
9. _____
10. _____
11. _____
12. _____
13. _____
14. _____
15. _____
16. _____
17. _____
18. _____
_____
19. _____
_____
20. _____
_____

128

WHAT YOU'VE LEARNED
Final

Date of Final_____

What have you learned through taking this course? This final will give you an opportunity to see how much you've learned while studying the material in this book. The purpose of this final is not to grade you, but to give you an opportunity to see what areas you need to work on.

1. _____ 26. _____
2. _____ 27. _____
3. _____ 28. _____
4. _____ 29. _____
5. _____ 30. _____
6. _____ 31. _____
7. _____ 32. _____
8. _____ 33. _____
9. _____ 34. _____
10. _____ 35. _____
11. _____ 36. _____
12. _____ 37. _____
13. _____ 38. _____
14. _____ 39. _____
15. _____ 40. _____
16. _____ 41. _____
17. _____ 42. _____
18. _____ 43. _____
19. _____ 44. _____
20. _____ 45. _____
21. _____ 46. _____
22. _____ 47. _____
23. _____ 48. _____
24. _____ 49. _____
25. _____ 50. _____